HOW TO GIVE EMPLOYEES PERFORMANCE FEEDBACK

& Resolve the Resistance You Know You're Going to Get!

OR

Feedback Skills for Everyday Situations and Performance Appraisal

» Give Employees Feedback the Way They *Want* to Receive It

» Successfully Resolve Resistance to Feedback

» Download Skill Practice Audio & Interactive Templates at www.PerformanceFeedbackTraining.com/skillpractice

ROSS BLAKE

Productive Work Relationships Publications

Chautauqua, New York

Give Feedback

⌄

Get Cooperation

⌄

Get Improvement

Contents

Product Disclaimer
This work is designed to provide accurate and authoritative information in regard to the subject matter covered. The author and publisher make no representation or warranties with respect to the accuracy, applicability, fitness, or completeness of the contents of this work. The information contained in this work is strictly for educational purposes. If you decide to apply ideas contained in this work, you are taking full responsibility for your actions.

The author and publisher disclaim any warranties (express or implied) as to merchantability, or fitness for any particular purpose. The author and publisher shall in no event be held liable to any party for any direct, indirect, punitive, special, incidental or other consequential damages arising directly or indirectly from any use of this work which is provided "as is," and without warranties.

ISBN 978-0-615-50184-0

Cover and interior design and layout by Sunny B. DiMartino

About the Author

Ross Blake is a senior level trainer and consultant who trains supervisors, managers, and HR professionals how to give employees performance feedback; resolve employee resistance to feedback; improve performance; and improve the work relationships between managers and employees.

In 1988, Ross Blake Associates, Inc started helping clients develop more effective supervisors, managers, and executives in team building, performance feedback, conflict resolution, employee retention, and leadership skills as well as executive coaching.

Several thousand training and consulting assignments were successfully completed for manufacturing and service organizations, including Bristol-Myers Squibb, Carrier Corporation, Corning Incorporated, Tyco Electronics, and other small and medium size organizations and educational institutions.

It's important to Ross that clients learn and apply actual skills instead of just reading or hearing about them; he delivers highly interactive, hands-on seminars, not power point lectures.

A passionate, and high-energy trainer, he encourages participants to contribute situations during training so that the skills being learned can directly be applied to them. His participants learn by demonstrations, discovery, participation, and skill practices, not lectures.

A graduate of Ohio University, he has also authored *How to Develop An Employee Retention Blueprint;* served as a program development and membership officer in several training and HR organizations; spoken before a number of human relations and business groups, and was the keynote speaker for an international talent management and consulting firm.

Ross resides in Chautauqua, NY, a center for the fine and performing arts, and enjoys international travel. People all over the world, he believes, are much more alike than they are different.

Give Feedback

˅

Get Cooperation

˅

Get Improvement

Introduction

Positive, Win-Win Skills to Give Feedback & Resolve Concerns

Effective feedback improves more than performance

Giving feedback is one of the most difficult things for managers to do, and for employees to receive. Using the skills in this manual, managers lose the fear of giving feedback, and employees lose the fear of receiving it, because they're both part of positive dialogues and the development of solutions.

The ability to give employees feedback while increasing their cooperation and reducing resentment, is an invaluable skill for all managers to have, and makes them more promotable.

One of the things I discovered working with managers and their employees was that the more effectively managers gave feedback, the more employees improved their performance, and the more some other very important things improved as well.

Among them were improved communication and the work relationships between managers and employees, where far more concerns and conflicts were resolved; collaboration increased; a better understanding of each other's expectations and work style occurred; and the results they accomplished together increased.

Unlike other feedback training tools in 4 key ways

While there are a number of seminars and books that provide good models for giving employees performance feedback, there are four ways the skills in this manual are different and superior:

1. **You'll learn to use the performance feedback model your employees *want* you to use with them (and that you *want* your boss to use with you)** The result is far more comfort and commitment in using these skills because you can relate to and believe in them.

2. **You'll learn 3 skills to successfully resolve employee resistance to feedback** Many managers learn feedback models, and then become discouraged when employees respond with resistance or excuses; they get stuck because they weren't trained how to respond. So they stop using the feedback skills, and allow concerns to continue, often until a boiling point results in an argument.

3. **You'll learn how to make performance agreements with employees in** *advance* **to avoid confrontations**
   Make agreements with employees in advance about how feedback will be given and received, and greatly reduce problems.

4. **You'll know what to do when employees agree to improve their performance and don't**
   A low-confrontation skill to put responsibility for agreement and implementation where it belongs-with the employee.

Now you'll be able to help employees *want* to collaborate because it's to their benefit to do so.

Giving feedback is the core skill needed to resolve everyday performance situations, and to conduct performance appraisals

This is the key skill this manual delivers, whether you need to correct everyday situations such as arriving for work late, not following procedures, spreading negative gossip, or conducting performance reviews.

Developed with input from 1,000s of professionals just like you

The easy-to-learn skills in this manual were created after 10 years of consulting, coaching, and training projects with several thousand team leaders, supervisors, and managers just like you in service and manufacturing organizations of all types and sizes.

These skills were developed, tested, and refined with their input and feedback after their use of the skills with their employees, so they're based on what's proven to be effective.

You learn actual skills, not just read or hear about them

Many books and seminars tell you about feedback skills without actually training you in feedback skills which this book does.

Skills are spelled out step-by-step in easy-to-learn formulas, in 4 steps or less

And, the small number of key skills you'll learn will likely help you resolve 80% or more of the situations you encounter instead of having to learn multiple skills for multiple situations.

Compatible with other performance management and leadership efforts

All of the skills and concepts in this manual are highly compatible with, and will typically enhance, other leadership training or performance evaluation and appraisal programs you may be using.

Download complete skill practice forms and audio at www.PerformanceFeedbackTraining.com/skillpractice

Skill practice forms are at the end of each chapter and downloadable at www.PerformanceFeedbackTraining.com/skillpractice. Hear the skills, then use the forms to script your actual situations and skill practice them. Plus, see the chapter about how best to learn your new skills.

It's rewarding

The skills in this manual will help you work in the ways you've most wanted to with your employees—with increased communication, comfort, collaboration, synergy, and results.

The term "manager" is used inclusively

The skills in this manual were developed to help anyone who needs to give one or more employees performance feedback. Although the term "manager" is used most often, it's intended to include all managerial positions, including forepersons, team leaders, work group leaders, supervisors, managers, executives, HR professionals, and business owners.

Next, the entire model.

Give Feedback

⌄

Get Cooperation

⌄

Get Improvement

Chapter 1

The Entire Model: How to Give Employees Performance Feedback & Resolve Resistance

If you're like me, you like to see the big picture in advance, so here's a summary of the skills you'll learn step-by-step in order to give employees feedback and resolve resistance.

How to Give Employees Performance Feedback: "2 Whats, 2 Whys & A Check Out:"

> » **Set the Stage for Win-Win**

1. Tell **WHAT** Needs Correcting

   & WHY

2. Tell **WHAT** You Want Instead

   & WHY

3. **Check Out**

   » Thank/Confirm

Resolve Resistance to Feedback Skill: Repeat-Answer-Repeat

1. **Repeat Their Concern**

   » No matter what their response is or how valid it is.

2. **Answer Their Concern**

   Option #1: Meet a Standard + Action You'll Take

   Option #2: Facilitate the Employee to Develop a Solution

3. **Repeat What/Why #2**

   » Repeat the What/Why#2 step from the Performance Feedback Skill.

That's it!

Give Feedback

﹀

Get Cooperation

﹀

Get Improvement

Chapter 2

How to Successfully Learn & Apply These Skills

They're Like Everything Else You've Ever Learned to Do Well

First, I make this promise to everyone reading this: you're already capable of successfully learning and applying these skills.

It's not difficult to learn them; all of them consist of a simple series of just 3 or 4 steps. In total, there are 5 simple skills to learn that'll resolve over 80% of the feedback situations you'll encounter.

However, just like anything else that you've ever learned to do well, you're going to have to work at learning these, including practicing them.

Here's the good news, though. These skills are not like learning to play the violin where you have to practice for months, even years, to begin to become sort of good.

Instead, most managers learning these skills report they notice improvement in their ability each time they practice or use them.

This means you can learn them fairly quickly.

Learn *One* Skill At a Time

Read through the entire manual once, making notes and underlines, and adding sticky notes and bookmarks, etc.

Then go back and master one skill at a time. Don't try to learn all of them at once; even though they're short and simple, you'll likely be overwhelmed if you do.

Download the audio at www.PerformanceFeedbackTraining.com/skillpractice and *hear* each skill demonstrated as you *visually* read the model, then *write* out your situation, and then *read, speak* and *hear* your situation as you skill practice it. Complete skill practice forms are at the end of each chapter and are downloadable as interactive templates at the website address above.

3 Methods to Skill Practice the Skills:
Good, Better, and *Best*

Method #1, *Good*: Skill Practice Them Yourself or At Home

Download audio and skill practice forms at www.PerformanceFeedbackTraining.com/skillpractice where you'll *see, hear, write,* and *speak* the skills until you're competent and comfortable at using them.

Give Yourself This Feedback:

» **How you would respond if you were the employee receiving the feedback.**

» **What you did well.**

» **How you can improve the next time.**

Also, find a friend or skill practice partner at home (including teenagers); have them give you the above feedback, and work with them until you're competent.

Method #2, *Better*: Skill Practice with a Colleague at Work

The colleague plays the role of an employee you're giving feedback to, while you play the role of the manager. This is highly beneficial because your colleague may be familiar with the feedback situations you face, and how employees typically respond.

Skill practice again and again, and have them give you the feedback in Method #1.

Method #3, *Best*: Two of You at Work Learn the Skills Together

This way, you get all of the benefits of having a colleague as mentioned above, plus the insights and observations of two people learning the same skills at the same time. Plus, it's a known fact that the more you help teach another person a skill, the more you'll learn that skill.

Both of you skill practice until you're competent, and each of you gives the other the feedback listed in Method #1.

This way you'll now have two smart people instead of one with these skills in your organization.

A Word of Advice

Don't make the *first* person you use your new skills with the most difficult employee in the organization; instead, make your first attempts with others.

Chapter 3

The Basics for Giving Performance Feedback

It's not only important **what** you say when you give employees feedback, it's also important **how** you say it.

7 Tips for Preparing and Conducting Feedback Sessions

1. **Practice what you're going to say** in advance, using the skills in this manual.

2. **Anticipate potential employee resistance or excuses**, and practice answering them, using the Repeat-Answer-Repeat skills.

3. **Talk in private when giving feedback;** it's amazing how often this isn't done.

4. **Get rid of physical barriers between you**, get out from behind desks or other objects, sit on chairs facing employees, or sit on the same side of a table with your chairs turned to face each other.

5. **It's the emotion in your voice that carries the freight**; emotion has a strong impact on people; use a calm and neutral tone of voice, neither aggressive nor submissive.

6. **Leave out anger, blame, criticism, sarcasm and accusations**; these only make employees angry and defensive. Remember that your end objective is to get cooperation and a resolution that's mutually-beneficial if possible; using negative or condescending language won't achieve this.

7. **Use open body language** when sitting or standing, including having your arms and legs uncrossed, and being a comfortable distance apart; nod your head occasionally; make eye contact from time-to-time; don't allow distractions.

8. **Use the Reflective Listening skill** to confirm understanding, avoid errors, and defuse emotions as you talk; Chapter 8 teaches you this skill.

Give Feedback

﹀

Get Cooperation

﹀

Get Improvement

Chapter 4

"Constructive Criticism" Isn't

You've more than likely heard other people use the term "constructive criticism" as in "he just doesn't know how to take constructive criticism well," or, "I think it's time to give her some constructive criticism."

Whoever thought of this term was well-intentioned, thinking that placing "constructive" in front of the word "criticism" would cancel it out.

But it doesn't, and this phrase turns or scares most people off.

"Constructive Criticism" Isn't Constructive

Think about this: if someone says, "Hey, do you want some "constructive criticism?" what's the *one word* you (and others) hear more than any other?

Right, it's "criticism." And most people already have all of the criticism they need or want.

Use "Performance Feedback" or "Constructive Feedback" Instead

From now on, let's use the terms "performance feedback" or "constructive feedback."

What is "feedback?"

It's simply information, without any negative labels, history, connotations or meanings.

And, it's much more likely to help both the giver and the receiver of feedback to feel more at ease. (This is important, because most people feel uncomfortable about giving and receiving feedback).

From now on, when our purpose is to help anyone improve their performance, we'll use "performance feedback."

Give Feedback

∨

Get Cooperation

∨

Get Improvement

Chapter 5

Four Factors That Make it Possible for Employees to Receive Performance Feedback and Cooperate

Or, what we can apply from learning to swim, golf, or ride a bicycle, to performance feedback.

a. Think of a time when you were learning to do something new, such as how to play golf, ride a bike, swim, etc.

b. From time-to-time, the person teaching you probably gave you some positive feedback about what you were doing well, such as, "Great job, you're keeping the bike balanced, and going straight ahead."

   » You more than likely felt good about receiving this feedback.

c. In addition, the person teaching you probably gave you some constructive feedback about something you needed to change, do differently, or improve such as, "Okay, watch where you're going, keep your handlebars straight, and use your brakes sooner."

   » You probably felt good (or at least okay) about receiving this feedback, even though it was about something you needed to change, improve, correct, or do differently.

It's understandable that you felt good about receiving positive feedback, most of us do.

But what made it possible for you to also feel good or at least okay about receiving performance or constructive feedback?

» Chances are, it was due to one or more of the "four feedback factors" on the next page.

Feedback Factor #1: The person giving you the feedback was knowledgeable.

They knew the subject they were giving you feedback about, and had observed you so they also knew what was happening.

Feedback Factor #2: The person's *intention* was to help you, not hurt you.

You could tell the person was trying to help you, not criticize you or put you down; they wanted you to succeed.

Feedback Factor #3: There was balance: they gave you both performance feedback and positive feedback.

The feedback they gave you wasn't only about the things you needed to change or improve.

They also gave you positive feedback, or praise, whenever you earned it, even if it was something small that you did correctly.

Hearing positive feedback in addition to performance feedback makes it much easier to listen to and act on things we need to change or improve. (More about this later.)

Feedback Factor #4: It was the way they said it.

This included their tone of voice, body language and facial expressions; how they spoke their words (did they "spit" them out in an angry or derogatory manner, or did they speak them politely, and firmly?)

What this demonstrates is highly important

All of us have received positive feedback about our performance, and felt good about it.

All of us have also received performance feedback about our performance, and have at least felt okay about it, because of how it was done.

This demonstrates that it's possible for people to receive feedback about the things they need to correct, change or improve—and still be able to feel okay—or even good about it—if it's done in the right way!

This is exactly what we're going to learn.

Chapter 6

The Purpose of Performance Feedback

The overriding purpose of giving performance feedback is to *help employees improve their performance* in order to improve their value to the organization, its customers, other employees, and themselves.

The Purpose of Giving Performance Feedback

1. To gain the employee's cooperation.
2. To get a resolution for the performance that needs to be corrected or improved.
3. To resolve related concerns the employee may have.
4. To help the employee improve their performance.
5. To maintain a good work relationship between the employee and his or her manager.

Give Feedback

⌄

Get Cooperation

⌄

Get Improvement

Chapter 7

How to Give Employees Performance Feedback Skill: "2 Whats, 2 Whys, & A Check Out"

The Contents of This Chapter

How to Give Employees Performance Feedback Skill: "2 Whats, 2 Whys, & A Check Out:"

Look at the How to Give Performance Feedback model again:

> » **Set the Stage for Win-Win**
>
> 1. Tell **WHAT** Needs Correcting
>   **& WHY**
>
> 2. Tell **WHAT** You Want Instead
>   **& WHY**
>
> 3. **Check Out**
>   » Thank/Confirm

See the "2 Whats, 2 Whys, & A Check Out" above?

Now we'll apply it to an actual work situation on the next page.

Applying the Performance Feedback Model to a Work Situation

A supervisor gives an employee feedback about not wearing safety glasses on the plant floor. Sound familiar?

Here's the Skill Model with Dialogue Examples and a Rationale below:

Skill Model: **Dialogue Example:**

» **Set the Stage for Win-Win**   **"I have a concern I'd like to share with you."**

» The manager says, "I have a concern I'd like to share with you," to let the employee know something important needs to be discussed, but it won't be a chewing out session.

» Why does the manager say "concern" instead of "problem?" "Problem" is negative, as in "You got a problem?" Or, "What's your problem?" A "concern" is more neutral; something to be discussed.

Tell **WHAT** Needs Correcting   **"When I see you not wearing safety glasses on the plant floor...**

» In the first WHAT above, the manager calmly describes the employee's behavior without using blame, anger, attack, or criticism.
In this case, it's "When I see you not wearing safety glasses on the plant floor..."

» Why does the manager say "When I see you not wearing safety glasses..." instead of saying "When **you** don't wear safety glasses?" Because "you" sounds like more of an accusation, and may trigger defensiveness.

& WHY   **"...it means you could be seriously injured."**

» In Why #1 above, the manager tells the employee *why* their behavior is a concern: "...**it means** you could be seriously injured." This states the *negative consequence* of the employee's behavior.

» What you hear in this step is "description," not "accusation."

Tell WHAT You Want Instead   **"I'd appreciate it if* you'd always wear your safety glasses in this area..."**

» In the second WHAT above, the manager tells the employee what they want them to do instead.

» In this case it's "I'd appreciate it if you'd always wear your safety glasses in this area..."

*This is spoken as a request: "I'd appreciate it if..." Other options are: "I'd like you to..." or, "Would you please..." More assertive is "I need to have you..."

& WHY   **"...so that you stay healthy and we avoid punitive fines."**

» In Why #2 above, the manager tells the employee *why* she wants them to do what she has requested.

This also states the *positive consequence* of meeting her request. In this case, it's "so you stay healthy and we avoid punitive fines."

Check Out   **"Any concerns about what I'm asking?"**

» The manager says: **"Any concerns about what I'm asking?"**

This opens the door for the employee to share a concern if they have one so it can be resolved. (Don't fear asking this; see Appendix A).

This step makes 2-way communication or dialogue possible, and gives the employee an opportunity to ask questions, provide input, solutions, etc.

» Don't ask "Do you understand?" or "Do you have a problem with this?" They're close-ended questions that are less likely to elicit concerns or information.

Employee   *"No."*

» Thank

» If the employee has no concerns and agrees to do what's asked, thank them and move on.

Optional:

» **Confirm If Necessary**	**"Do I have your agreement?"**
Employee	*"Yes."*
» **Thank**	**"Thanks."**

The manager asks if s/he has the employee's agreement if past history suggests the need to confirm agreements with them. If not, skip it.

You'll Get One of Two Responses After Using the Check Out Step Question: "Any Concerns About What I'm Asking?"

Response #1: Agreement

The employee doesn't have a concern, agrees to cooperate, and the matter is resolved.

» **Thank him or her, and move on.**

Response #2: Resistance

The employee responds with excuses, a laundry list of complaints, accusations of being singled out, defensiveness, etc.

The next two skills will help you resolve employee resistance to feedback.

» *A Skill Practice form for this skill begins on the next page.*

Skill Practice A: How to Give Employees Performance Feedback Skill: "2 Whats, 2 Whys & A Check Out"

» In this practice, the employee doesn't respond with a concern to the step 3 question, "Any concerns about what I'm asking?"

» Write a situation using the How to Give Employees Performance Feedback skill on this form.

» Or, download an interactive template of this form at www.PerformanceFeedback Training.com/skillpractice.

» Set the Stage for Win-Win

(Write below: "I have a concern I'd like to share with you.")

1 Tell **WHAT** Needs Correcting

"When I...

& WHY

(Why it's a concern; its negative consequence)

2   Tell **WHAT** You Want Instead

"I'd appreciate it if...

_____

_____

_____

_____

& WHY

(Why you want this instead; its positive consequence)

_____

_____

_____

3   Check Out

(Write below: "Any concerns about what I'm asking?")

_____

» Thank

(Sometimes, employees won't have a concern, and will agree to do what you've asked; write "Thank you" below)

_____

Optional:

If past history with this employee suggests the need to confirm agreements with them, use this step; if not, skip it.

» **"Do I have your agreement?"** _("Yes.")_ **"Thanks."**

Give Feedback

⌄

Get Cooperation

⌄

Get Improvement

Chapter 8

The Skill to Resolve Employee Resistance to Performance Feedback: Repeat-Answer-Repeat

Answer Their Concern Option #1: Meet a Standard + Action You'll Take

When employees respond with a concern after the manager asks, "Any concerns about what I'm asking?" in step 3, the Check Out step, here's how to resolve their concern no matter how valid it is or isn't.

There are 2 options in the "Answer Their Concern" step; this is Option #1, Meet a Standard + Action You'll Take.

The Contents of This Chapter

» Answer Their Concern Option #1: Meet a Standard + Action You'll Take

» How to Do the "Repeat Their Concern" Step

» What "Answer Their Concern" Is and Is Not

» How to Develop Standards + Action You'll Take

» Skill Practice Form

Answer Their Concern Option # 1:
Meet a Standard + Action You'll Take

When to Use This Skill: *based on the concern the employee gives you,* use this option when a situation is best resolved by the manager upholding an organizational or work standard, plus an action s/he will take.

The Skill to Resolve Employee Resistance to Feedback:
Repeat-Answer-Repeat, Option #1:

1. **Repeat Their Concern ("What you're saying is...")**
   » No matter what their response is or how valid it is.

2. **Answer Their Concern: Meet a Standard + Action You'll Take**

3. **Repeat What/Why #2**
   » Repeat the What/Why #2 step from the Performance Feedback Skill.

» Let's go back to What/Why#2 to the How to Give Performance Feedback skill in the previous chapter where the supervisor said to the employee:

Tell **WHAT** You Want Instead	**"I'd appreciate it if you'd always wear your safety glasses in this area...**
& WHY	**...so that you stay healthy and we avoid punitive fines."**
» Check Out	**"Any concerns about what I'm asking?"**
Employee	*"You're just singling me out, giving me a hard time. Hey, why don't you ever go after Pete and Billy, they don't wear their safety glasses!*

» Here's how the manager responds:

1 Repeat Their Concern	**"What you're saying is you think I'm just picking on you—and giving Pete and Billy a free ride."**

Employee	*"Yes."*

» The manager repeats the employee's concern: **"What you're saying is** you think I'm just picking on you—and giving Pete and Billy a free ride." (Employee: "Yes.")

» This confirms that the manager correctly understood what the employee said; demonstrates to the employee that they've been heard; and helps defuse emotion and build cooperation. Repeat any concern an employee gives you, no matter how valid or invalid it seems. (See FAQ #2).

2 Answer Their Concern

» Meet a Standard	**"It's important to me that we work safely. This means that all of us, including me, must wear safety glasses to avoid injuries, to keep product moving, and to avoid punitive fines."**

» The manager thinks of a valid work, safety, ethical, or organizational standard to uphold and expands on it. The standard the manager chose is related to, and helps answer, the employee's concern.

» Start by saying: **"It's important to me..."** (In this case, the manager says, "It's important to me that we work safely.")

» This provides a valid reason for what the manager is requesting; shows the manager isn't just pulling rank; and is difficult to argue with.

» + Action You'll Take	**"I promise you, in fact, I guarantee you, that as soon as I see anyone not wearing safety glasses, I'm going to be there on top of it. If the President of the US shows up on my shift, s/he's going to have to wear safety glasses!"**

» The manager takes the first step, and thinks of an action s/he can take to help resolve the employee's concern, and move forward. (In this case, the manager promises she'll talk to anyone not wearing safety glasses).

Repeat What/Why #2	"I'd appreciate it if you'd always wear your safety glasses in this area...so that you stay healthy and we avoid punitive fines."

» The manager repeats (or reasserts) her original request in the Tell What You Want Instead & Why step (What/Why #2) to prompt the employee to agree and move forward.

In this case, it's "I'd appreciate it if you'd always wear your safety glasses in this area... ...so you stay healthy and we avoid punitive fines."

» Thank	"Thanks."

Optional:

» **Confirm If Necessary**	**"Do I have your agreement?"**
Employee	*"Yes."*
» **Thank**	**"Thanks."**

The manager asks if s/he has the employee's agreement if past history suggests the need to confirm agreements with them. If not, skip it.

Extent of the Manager's Role

The manager initiates an appropriate action to help resolve the employee's concern, with the employee still responsible for proper performance.

What Most Employees Will Do Next

Unless there's another issue they feel strongly about, or they want to test you by bringing up multiple issues, most employees will agree to do what you've asked.

What If an Employee Brings Up More Concerns or Excuses Again and Again?

You repeat the same 3 steps (Repeat Their Concern; Answer Their Concern; Repeat What/Why#2) as many times as it takes—until there's a resolution.

How to Do the "Repeat Their Concern" Step

In the third step of the How to Give Performance Feedback Skill, the manager uses the Check Out question, "Any concerns about what I'm asking?"

If the employee responds with a concern, the first step is to *repeat back in your own words the key points or highlights of the concern the employee gave you* no matter how valid their concern is or isn't.

Here's an example of using **Repeat Their Concern:**

| » **Check Out** | **"Any concerns about what I'm asking?"** |
| Employee | *"You're just singling me out, giving me a hard time. Hey, why don't you ever go after Pete and Billy, they don't wear their safety glasses!* |

| **Repeat Their Concern** | **"What you're saying is you think I'm just picking on you—and giving Pete and Billy a free ride."** |

| Employee | *"Yes."* |

» The manager used a "Starter Phrase" to begin her response, and then repeated only the highlights of what the employee said:

"What you're saying is…" *("Starter Phrase")*

You think I'm just picking on you—and giving Pete and Billy a free ride."
(Repeated the highlights of what the employee said)

» She repeated the *highlights* of what the employee said, but not everything the employee said. This confirms that the manager correctly heard the employee's concern which helps increase cooperation and reduce defensiveness. (Some readers may recognize this as the Reflective Listening skill).

*You can vary the Starter Phrase with: "If I heard you correctly…" or "What I'm hearing you say is…"

Another example:

» **Check Out**   **"Any concerns about what I'm asking?"**

Employee   *"My stupid car is old and doesn't always start in the morning so I can't get to work on time. Plus, it probably needs some repairs."*

| 1 | Repeat Their Concern | **"What you're saying is... your car isn't always dependable so you can get to work on time, and it needs repairs."** |

Employee   *"Yes."*

» The employee will typically say "yes" to confirm that you've heard them correctly.

"Repeat Their Concern" Skill Practice

Here's an employee concern. Write down how you'd "repeat it back" beginning with this Starter Phrase: "What you're saying is..."

Employee Concern: *"It's not that big of a deal, I wasn't gone that long to tell her how the show ended last night. Besides, the machinery should stop making product if it jams or there's a safety problem."*

Repeat Their Concern:

"What you're saying is...

_____

_____

_____

What "Answer Their Concern" Is and Is Not

Some managers think they're using this skill when they provide an answer or response of almost any sort to an employee's concern.

However, just "giving an answer" (or redirecting the employee elsewhere), is not what this skill is about.

It's about "giving an answer" that resolves the situation; that may involve creative thinking and problem solving by the manager and/or the employee; and that, as often as possible, is mutually-agreeable.

This is hard work; but it can pay off tremendously by resolving problems, and gaining increased employee cooperation and efforts to improve their performance.

An Example of What "Answer Their Concern" Is Not:

Here's an actual situation and how a manager not "answering their concern" would have responded.

Situation: *An employee wants to take 2 weeks (10 days) of vacation during the month of December for a family reunion in England. However, company policy states that employees cannot take more than two vacation days in December because it's the company's busy season.*

Manager: "I'm sorry, but the rules are the rules; the company handbook clearly states that employees cannot take more than two vacation days during the month of December because it's our busy season."

» The manager is technically correct, and has "answered" the employee.

But has the manager truly done everything she or he can do to "answer the concern" the employee has?

How happy or satisfied would you have been with this response?

And how might it affect your job performance in the future?

An Example of What "Answer Their Concern" Is:

Here's how a manager at a major Northeastern US dairy food manufacturing plant actually responded to this situation.

Manager:

» **Meet a Standard:** "It's important to me that employees get time off if possible when they need it, or if they have a special request. I want all of us to feel good about working here."

» **+ Action You'll Take:** "As you know, the company handbook states that employees cannot take more than two vacation days during the month of December because we're super busy then trying to keep up with customer orders."

"You're a hard-working employee, plus you've helped me when I've been short-handed. What I can do is go to my boss, the Plant Manager, and discuss this with him. If the December work schedule permits, every consideration will be given to your special request based on the company's employee performance and reward system."

» **Note that this manager more fully "Answers Their Concern"** by thinking about the employee's request *instead of just quickly finding a way to answer it by rejecting it,* and also *determines what action s/he can take, and does it. You may need to think more creatively than you have in the past to answer concerns.*

How much happier or more satisfied would you be with this answer?

And how might it affect your job performance in the future?

Do you think you'd like to work for this manager?

How to Develop Standards

Here's how to develop the 2 key components of the Answer Their Concern: Meet a Standard + Action You'll Take skill beginning with Meet a Standard.

What are "Good Standards?"

They're important operating principles, values, objectives, or ways of working that managers and employees need to follow or achieve for the well-being of other employees, customers, and the entire organization.

In addition, they help form the rationale for what the manager asks the employee to do differently.

Characteristics of Good Standards:

» Fair and reasonable.

» Help to meet individual, team, managerial, organizational objectives.

» Usually apply to everyone's benefit; standards are not one-sided or demands to "work harder."

» Are stated in terms of their positive benefit or result.

» Are safe, legal and ethical.

» Are difficult to argue with or oppose.

For example: Who can argue with working safely or meeting customer needs so their business is retained? Or working with other employees agreeably so everyone works comfortably and productively?

Examples of "Good Standards Statements"

"It's important that we help co-workers when they're overloaded so no one gets injured or overworked."

"It's necessary that we're all here at the beginning of the shift so we get the latest customer specs in order to meet them."

"It's important to me that we share information with each other so we avoid making errors, and the time it takes to correct them."

Where Do You Find "Good Standards" in *Your* Organization?

Almost everywhere: here are over 30 of them in 5 different categories. But wait; you can no doubt create more!

1. **Standards involving customers:**

   » meeting customer specifications,

   » shipping complete orders,

   » meeting deadlines,

   » retaining customers,

   » increasing the amount of their business,

   » responding promptly and courteously,

   » learning new customer needs to better compete with competitors.

2. **Standards involving other employees:**

   » help all feel comfortable so we work together productively,

   » help others out when they're overloaded so we get the job done without anyone being overwhelmed,

   » acknowledge and greet each other so no one feels ignored,

   » treat each other with respect so we can focus on work objectives instead of staff issues,

   » not gossip or badmouth others, hurting their performance,

   » instead of complaining about other people, we go to them and work out concerns agreeably,

   » all of us get recognized for solid or outstanding work.

3. **Standards involving safety so that:**

   » no one is injured or requires medical treatment,

   » no one is killed, creating grief for their families,

   » customer shipments aren't missed,

   » punitive fines and write ups are not incurred,

   » insurance costs are not increased,

   » lost time accidents are avoided,

» fires are avoided,

» good potential employees want to apply to work here,

» we can continue to afford health insurance, etc.

4. **Standards involving physical plant so that:**

   » our equipment operates safely,

   » customer shipments aren't delayed,

   » machinery runs because we do preventive maintenance,

   » unnecessary repairs aren't incurred leaving money for better things,

   » utility expenses are lowered.

5. **Standards involving productivity so that we:**

   » avoid layoffs or make them much less likely,

   » can hire more employees as needed,

   » maintain or increase wages,

   » maintain or increase benefits such as health insurance,

   » do not lose business to competitors,

   » have money for necessary plant improvements,

   » can out produce our competitors,

   » don't have some employees doing more than their fair share of work or all of the hard or dirty tasks,

   » retain our customers, increase our value to them, and increase their business.

You get the idea.

How to Develop Actions You'll Take

Now, develop Actions You'll Take to go with each Standard.

What is an "Action You'll Take?"

It's something that you as the manager can do in order to help answer or resolve a concern an employee gives you.

Characteristics of Good "Actions You'll Take"

» They're specific and clear about action(s) to be taken.

» They're often stated with some energy, passion or commitment.

» They can be measured or observed.

» They get something started that helps resolve the concern.

Examples of Other "Actions You'll Take" Statements

"I promise you I'll make a genuine effort to notice the projects you're doing well, to thank you, and to see that a report goes into your personnel file."

"I'll be certain you have the fire retardant gloves you need to do the job safely, and I'll have them sent by express air tonight; plus, I'll get extra pairs."

"I guarantee you that if I hear other employees making negative comments about anyone else, I'll stop and talk with them as well."

How to Think of "Actions You Can Take" Statements

Develop several Standards, and then write an "Action You'll Take" that helps meet them.

Write A Standard + Action You'll Take Skill Practice

Write a Standard + An Action You'll Take for the situation below as a skill practice.

Situation: You're Just Picking on Me

An employee is arriving for work late, putting a heavier work load on other employees, and delaying the on-time delivery of products to customers.

You've used the performance feedback skill to ask him to be at work on time.

In response to "Any concerns about what I'm asking," he said:

"Why are you only talking to me? Frank and Kathy arrive for work late a lot!"

» Using this situation, write a Meet a Standard statement + Action You'll Take:

1. **Meet a Standard:** *What's a standard from your workplace that applies here?* Write it as: **"It's important that..."**

   _____

   _____

   _____

   _____

   _____

2. **+ An Action You'll Take:** *Write an action you can take to help resolve this.*

   _____

   _____

   _____

   _____

   _____

» *A Skill Practice form for the entire skill begins on the next page.*

Skill Practice B: How to Give Employees Performance Feedback AND Resolve Employee Resistance to Feedback: Repeat-Answer-Repeat

Answer Their Concern Option #1: Meet a Standard + Action You'll Take

» The How to Give Employees Performance Feedback Skill has been combined with this Resolve Employee Resistance to Feedback Skill so you can practice resolving resistance to feedback using just one form.

» Write a DIFFERENT feedback situation for the How to Give Employees Performance Feedback Skill below, one that's best resolved by the manager upholding an organizational or work standard, plus an action s/he will take. (If the situation you used on the skill practice form at the end of Chapter 7 applies here, you can use it).

» Or, download an interactive template of this form at www.PerformanceFeedback Training.com/skillpractice.

(How to Give Performance Feedback Skill)

> **» Set the Stage for Win-Win**

(Write below: "I have a concern I'd like to share with you.")

> **1   Tell WHAT Needs Correcting**

"When I...

_____

_____

_____

38

How to Give Employees Performance Feedback
AND Resolve Employee Resistance to Feedback: Page 1
Repeat-Answer-Repeat Option #1 Skill Practice B

& WHY

(Why it's a concern; its negative consequence)

_____

_____

_____

_____

2 Tell **WHAT** You Want Instead

"I'd appreciate it if...

_____

_____

_____

_____

& WHY

(Why you want this instead; its positive consequence)

_____

_____

_____

_____

3 Check Out

(Write below: "Any concerns about what I'm asking?")

_____

Page 2 | How to Give Employees Performance Feedback
AND Resolve Employee Resistance to Feedback:
Repeat-Answer-Repeat Option #1 Skill Practice B

39

(Resolve Resistance to Feedback: Repeat-Answer-Repeat Skill)

Employee's Concern:
(Write a concern an employee might give you in response to the question "Any concerns about what I'm asking?")

_____

_____

_____

_____

1 **Repeat Their Concern**

(Write down how you'd repeat the employee's concern.)
"What you're saying is...

_____

_____

_____

2 **Answer Their Concern: Meet a Standard + Action You'll Take**

» Meet a Standard

(Write one or more standards you want to meet)
"It's important...

_____

_____

_____

_____

_____

40

How to Give Employees Performance Feedback
AND Resolve Employee Resistance to Feedback: | Page 3
Repeat-Answer-Repeat Option #1 Skill Practice B

» + Action You'll Take

(Write an action you can take)

_____

_____

_____

3 Repeat What/Why #2

(Write your original What/Why #2; it begins with "I'd appreciate it if…").

_____

_____

_____

_____

_____

Optional:

If past history with this employee suggests the need to confirm agreements with them, use this step; if not, skip it.

» **"Do I have your agreement?"** *("Yes.")* **"Thanks."**

Page 4 | How to Give Employees Performance Feedback AND Resolve Employee Resistance to Feedback: Repeat-Answer-Repeat Option #1 Skill Practice B

41

Give Feedback

⌄

Get Cooperation

⌄

Get Improvement

Chapter 9

The Skill to Resolve Employee Resistance to Performance Feedback: Repeat-Answer-Repeat

Answer Their Concern Option #2: Facilitate the Employee to Develop a Solution

When employees respond with a concern after the manager asks, "Any concerns about what I'm asking?" in step 3, the Check Out step, here's another skill to resolve it.

There are 2 options in the "Answer Their Concern" step; this is Option #2, Facilitate the Employee to Develop a Solution.

The Contents of This Section

» Answer Their Concern Option #2: Facilitate the Employee to Develop a Solution

» How to Develop Questions to Facilitate Employees

» When to Use "Answer Their Concern" Option #1 or 2

» Skill Practice Form

Answer Their Concern Option #2:
Facilitate the Employee to Develop a Solution

When to use this skill: *based on the concern the employee gives you,* use this option when a situation is best resolved by the employee, such as arriving for work late. (It's their responsibility; plus, they know far more about their situation, and how to resolve it than you do).

The Skill to Resolve Employee Resistance to Performance Feedback: Repeat-Answer-Repeat, Option #2:

1. **Repeat Their Concern** ("What you're saying is...")

   » No matter what their response is or how valid it is.

2. **Answer Their Concern: Facilitate the Employee to Develop a Solution**

   » **What can you do to...?**

   » **What else could you do?**

   » **What *will* you do?**

3. **Repeat What/Why #2:**

   » Repeat the What/Why#2 step from the Performance Feedback Skill.

» Let's start with a new What/Why #2, where the supervisor says to the employee:

Tell **WHAT** You Want Instead	**"I'd appreciate it if you'd arrive for work on time at 7:00am...**
& WHY	**...so that our consumers get the meds they need, their families know we're taking good care of them, and none of us gets overloaded."**
» **Check Out**	**"Any concerns about what I'm asking?"**
Employee	*"My stupid car doesn't always start in the morning. It probably needs some repairs also."*

» Here's how the manager responds:

1	**Repeat Their Concern**	**"What you're saying is your car isn't always dependable so you can get to work on time."**

Employee	*"Yes."*

» The manager repeats the employee's concern: **"What you're saying is** your car isn't always dependable so you can get to work on time."

This confirms that the manager correctly understood what the employee said; demonstrates to the employee that they've been heard; and helps defuse emotion and build cooperation. Repeat all concerns, no matter how valid or invalid they seem.

2	**Answer Their Concern**	
	» Facilitate Employee	**"What can you do to get your car fixed or to get transportation so you arrive for work on time at 7:00am?"**

Employee	*"I could get an estimate for all of the repairs, and start getting some of them made."*
» Manager	**"What else could you do?"**
Employee	*"I could see if it's going to start 15 minutes before I leave and call someone else for a ride if it won't."*
» Manager	**"What else could you do?"**
Employee	*"I could borrow my brother's car; he doesn't go in till third shift."*
» Manager	**"What *will* you do?"**
Employee	*"I'll get some repairs started and borrow my brother's car if I have to."*

» The manager asks 3 questions to facilitate the employee in developing a solution:

"What can you do…to be certain you get to work on time?"** *(The desired end result for the employee)*

"What else could you do?" *(Asks 3–4 times to get a # of ideas)*

"What *will* you do?" *(To get a decision/plan)*

3	Repeat What/Why #2	"I'd appreciate it if you'd arrive for work on time at 7:00am…so that our consumers get the meds they need, their families know we're taking good care of them, and none of us gets overloaded."

» The manager repeats (or reasserts) her original request in the What You Want Instead & Why step (What/Why #2) to prompt the employee to agree and move forward.

In this case, it's **"I'd appreciate it** if you'd arrive for work on time at 7:00am… so that our consumers get the meds they need, their families know we're taking good care of them, and none of us gets overloaded."

Optional:

» **Confirm If Necessary**	**"Do I have your agreement?"**
Employee	*"Yes, I'll be there on time."*
» **Thank**	**"Thanks."**

The manager asks if s/he has the employee's agreement if past history suggests the need to confirm agreements with them. If not, skip it.

How to Develop Questions to Facilitate Employees

The first question in this model is the basis for *facilitating* employees in developing potential solutions.

Here's the Answer Their Concern Option #2 step again:

2. Answer Their Concern: Facilitate the Employee to Develop a Solution

> » **What can you do to...?**

> » **What else could you do? (Ask 3–4x)**

> » **What *will* you do?**

How to Develop the "What can you do to...?" Question to Help Employees Develop Solutions

Construct the first question ("What can you do to...") by combining what the manager wants the employee to do from What/Why #2 with the employee's concern.

For the situation we've been working on, here's what the manager wants the employee to do from What/Why #2:

"I'd appreciate it if you'd arrive for work on time at 7:00am (so that our consumers get the meds they need, their families know we're taking good care of them, and none of us gets overloaded.")

"Any concerns about what I'm asking?"

For the situation we've been working on, here's the employee's concern:

"My stupid car doesn't always start in the morning. It probably needs some repairs, also."

The first or problem-solving question for the employee now becomes:

"What can you do to get your car fixed or to get transportation so you arrive for work on time at 7:00am?"

> » Note that only the key objective of what the manager wants the employee to do in What/Why#2 is used: "arrive for work on time at 7:00am." (The rest of the sentence isn't needed.)

In a different situation, here's what the manager wants the employee to do from What/Why #2:

"I'd appreciate it if you'd arrive for work alert and ready to go, so you get the production line started on time and we ship complete customer orders."

"Any concerns about what I'm asking?"

The employee's concern:

"I have a little part time job on the side, so sometimes I'm not always well-rested when I come to work."

The first or problem-solving question for the employee is:

"What can you do to finish your part time job and be certain you're well-rested when you arrive for work here?"

Note that only the key objective of what the manager wants the employee to do in What/Why #2 is stated: "be certain you're well-rested when you arrive for work here." (This part, "so you get the production line started on time and we ship complete customer orders" isn't needed).

Skill Practice: Another situation:

In another situation, here's what the manager wants the employee to do from What/Why #2:

"I'd appreciate it if you'd make calls on your cell phone only during breaks and lunch periods so that customers aren't kept waiting, and we can serve them faster."

"Any concerns about what I'm asking?"

The employee's concern:

"Yes, my sister calls to keep me informed about how my father is doing with his new home health aide."

Skill Practice: Finish the "What can you do to…" question below using this situation: (See the bottom of the next page for a possible answer).

"What can you do to…

48

Don't Be Thrown Off Course with "I don't have an idea."

Sometimes you'll get this response after asking: "What can you do to..?"

Don't let it stop you, respond with: **"If you had an idea, what would it be?"**

When It's Okay to Give Ideas or Advice

Sometimes you may have a good solution that an employee hasn't thought of.

How can you suggest it without taking responsibility for their situation, or without providing unsolicited advice—which many people don't want and will reject?

If an employee hasn't thought of a good idea you have *after* you've first asked them, "What can you do to..." and "What else could you do?" then ask them:

"Want an idea?" Or, **"Want some advice?"**

Most people will say yes. Since you now have their permission, go ahead and give them your idea.

4 Tips for Using this Skill

Tip #1: Don't ask: "Do you have a solution?" because asking a "yes" or "no" question is more likely to get you a "no."

» Notice how the manager's first question, **"What can you do to...?** is an open-ended question for the employee to answer with several options.

Tip #2: Asking "What else could you do?" 3 to 4 times gets more options.

» Don't let them stop at just one idea, keep pumping them for several more.

Tip #3: Asking "What *will* you do?" leads to a decision and action.

Tip #4: Thank them when you get an agreeable solution.

» It helps employees commit to doing it, and shows you appreciate their cooperation.

(Possible Answer: "What can you do to stay informed about your father and his new aide, and not use your cell phone unless it's during breaks or lunch?")

When to Use "Answer Their Concern" Option #1 or # 2

Answer this question:

Based on the concern the employee gives you:

"Who can best resolve this situation?"

Choose Option #1 when a manager upholding and meeting a standard + an action they can take will best resolve the situation.

Choose Option #2 when an employee has the responsibility, and the most knowledge and control, to best resolve the situation (such as arriving for work on time; wearing safety shoes to work; getting transportation to work; having daycare service, etc.)

» *A Skill Practice form for the entire skill begins on the next page.*

Skill Practice C: How to Give Employees Performance Feedback AND Resolve Employee Resistance to Feedback: Repeat-Answer-Repeat

Answer Their Concern Option #2: Facilitate Employee to Develop a Solution

» Write a DIFFERENT feedback situation for the How to Give Employees Performance Feedback Skill, one that's best resolved by the employee, such as arriving for work late; forgetting to wear their safety shoes, etc. (It's their responsibility, plus they know far more about their situation, and how to resolve it, than you do).

» Or, download an interactive template of this form at www.PerformanceFeedback Training.com/skillpractice.

(How to Give Performance Feedback Skill)

» Set the Stage for Win-Win

(Write below: "I have a concern I'd like to share with you.")

Tell **WHAT** Needs Correcting

"When I...

Page 1 | How to Give Employees Performance Feedback AND Resolve Employee Resistance to Feedback: Repeat-Answer-Repeat Option #2 Skill Practice C

51

& WHY

(Why it's a concern; its negative consequence)

_____

_____

_____

_____

Tell **WHAT** You Want Instead

"I'd appreciate it if...

_____

_____

_____

_____

& WHY

(Why you want this instead; its positive consequence)

_____

_____

_____

_____

Check Out

(Write below: "Any concerns about what I'm asking?")

_____

52

How to Give Employees Performance Feedback
AND Resolve Employee Resistance to Feedback: | Page 2
Repeat-Answer-Repeat Option #2 Skill Practice C

(Resolve Resistance to Feedback: Repeat-Answer-Repeat Skill)

Employee's Concern:
(Write a concern an employee might give you in response to the question "Any concerns about what I'm asking?")

Repeat Their Concern

(Write down how you'd repeat the employee's concern.)
"What you're saying is...

Answer Their Concern: Facilitate the Employee

(Write the remainder of this question by combining the end result you want the employee to accomplish while addressing the employee's concern. For example: "What can you do to be here at 8:00 am (the end result) and see that your children arrive at school on time?" (employee's concern.)
"What can you do to...

Page 3 | How to Give Employees Performance Feedback
AND Resolve Employee Resistance to Feedback:
Repeat-Answer-Repeat Option #2 Skill Practice C

53

» **"What else could you do?"** *(Ask the employee this question)*

» **"What else could you do?"** *(Ask the employee this question again)*

» **"What else could you do?"** *(Ask the employee this question a third time)*

» **"What *will* you do?"** *(Ask this last question to get an action step from the employee)*

3 Repeat What/Why #2

(Write your original What/Why #2; it begins with "I'd appreciate it if…")

_____

_____

_____

_____

_____

_____

Optional:

If past history with this employee suggests the need to confirm agreements with them, use this step; if not, skip it.

» **"Do I have your agreement?"** *("Yes.")* **"Thanks."**

54

How to Give Employees Performance Feedback
AND Resolve Employee Resistance to Feedback: Page 4
Repeat-Answer-Repeat Option #2 Skill Practice C

Chapter 10

Summary of the Feedback and Resolve Resistance Skills

How to Give Performance Feedback: "2 Whats, 2 Whys & A Check Out:"

» **Set the Stage for Win-Win**

1. Tell **WHAT** Needs Correcting
   & WHY

2. Tell **WHAT** You Want Instead
   & WHY

3. **Check Out**
   » Thank/Confirm

How to Resolve Employee Resistance to Feedback: Repeat-Answer-Repeat

1. **Repeat Their Concern**
   » No matter what their response is or how valid it is.

2. **Answer Their Concern**
   Option #1: Meet a Standard +Action You'll Take
   Option #2: Facilitate the Employee to Develop a Solution

3. **Repeat What/Why #2**
   » Repeat the What/Why#2 step from the Performance Feedback Skill.

That's it!

Give Feedback

∨

Get Cooperation

∨

Get Improvement

Chapter 11

What If an Employee Agrees to Do Something, and Then Doesn't?

How to handle performance agreements that aren't kept

Sometimes employees make agreements to correct or improve something, and then they don't do it.

To resolve this, repeat the agreement you and the employee made; describe what happened instead, and ask the employee how come as shown below:

Skill Model:	Dialogue Example:
1. Repeat the Agreement	"When you and I met last Tuesday, you agreed you'd arrive for work on time at 7:00am."
2. Report What Happened Instead	"Today, I saw you arrive 20 minutes late, at 7:20am."
3. Ask	"How come?"

» **Notice that you don't hear blame, anger, attack, or accusations.** And that responsibility is placed right on the employee—where it belongs.

A New Agreement or Consequences? Your objective is to get a new agreement from the employee to do what they've promised. If their infraction is serious, or if this isn't the first time you've spoken to them, you can warn them of consequences if their non-compliance continues.

» If an employee makes a new agreement and breaks it again, use this skill again; then, depending on the validity of the employee's response, deliver consequences.

Performance Agreement Not Kept Skill Practice

Think of an agreement an employee made with you and didn't keep; write a script below using the "Ask" question ("How come?").

1. **Repeat The Agreement**

2. **Report What Happened Instead**

3. **Ask**

Chapter 12

Make Performance Feedback Agreements With Employees in *Advance*

What if you knew in advance how each employee wanted you to give them feedback so they'd be more likely to cooperate when you gave it to them?

It's a lot easier to get things done when people agree in advance how they'll do them.

Most managers know they need to give their employees feedback.

Most employees know their managers need to give them feedback.

Since both of them know this, why not have managers and employees create feedback agreements *in advance* that both of them can agree to and live with?

Here's the process:

1. **Tell Employees Your Intention About Delivering Feedback**

   "I want to be the type of manager who helps her/his people develop, and be of real value to the organization and themselves."

2. **Tell Employees Your Positive Feedback Philosophy**

   "I want to be sure I give you positive feedback about the things you do well in your job—and I'm sure there will be a lot of them."

3. **Tell Employees Your Performance Feedback Philosophy**

   "We're going to be working on lots of different projects. From time-to-time, I may need to give you some feedback about something you need to correct or how to improve something you're doing."

4. **Get the Employee's "How to Give Me Performance Feedback Model" and Write It Down**

   "If I need to give you feedback about something you need to improve or correct, how do you want me to give it to you so you don't feel dumped on, and can focus on making improvements?"

   "What steps do you want me to take? I'll list them right here."

   "What's another step you'd like me to take?"

   » Ask employees the above questions and <u>write down</u> *how they want you to give them feedback.*

   Tip: You may need to prompt them from time-to-time if they forget a feedback element you know is important, or that's included in the How to Give Performance Feedback Skill.

   For example, suppose they don't mention "*Why* you want me to do it this way instead?" (Or, Why #2).

   Say: "Okay, if I tell you what I want you to do instead, is there anything else you want to know about this?" (Most will say "tell me why.")

   If they don't mention this, ask them: "Do you want to know *why* I want you to do it this way instead?"

5. **Make a "Performance Feedback Agreement" with Each Employee**

   "Okay, I'm willing to give you feedback about your performance in the ways that you want it—if you're willing to cooperate when you receive it, work with me to resolve concerns, and make improvements."

   "Do we have a deal?"

» ***Action Step:*** Write out and practice these 5 steps until you can deliver them capably without notes.

What If They Don't Cooperate the Next Time They Receive Feedback?

Remind them about your agreement:

"When you and I spoke about my giving you feedback some time ago, you agreed that if I *(repeat what they agreed to),* you'd respond cooperatively. Is there something else I need to do to help you do this?"

Most employees will respond cooperatively; sometimes, there may be an issue or concern that needs to be resolved first.

Chapter 13

How to Give Positive Feedback Effectively

"No one in any organization has ever complained to me that their boss gives them too much sincere praise and appreciation!"

—Ross Blake

One of the Most Powerful But Least Used Managerial Skills There Is: Giving Positive Feedback

Research over the years has shown again and again that what employees want most in the workplace is appreciation for a job well done.

Exactly what is "appreciation for a job well done?" It's a thank you.

When employees do things right or well, thank them, even if it's for doing the job they're being paid to do. Why? Because it will help them want to continue doing whatever you've praised them about—and prompt them to look for other things to do well and receive praise about, and on and on.

Here's the 2 step skill to give positive feedback:

1. Thank	**"Jolene, thank you for the great job you did on the Wilson project."**
2. Tell WHY	**"You finished it a week ahead of time and $600.00 below budget."**

» What does thanking Jolene encourage her to do?

1. To continue to finish projects ahead of time and below budget.

2. It also prompts her to look for other things to do well because she now knows her boss looks for and recognizes good work. (How many times have you ever said or heard someone else say "Nobody ever notices or appreciates what I do?")

Four Important Rules About Giving Positive Feedback

Rule #1: Be Sincere

Never say it if you don't mean it! You know before you speak it if you truly mean it or not. You can get away with flattering people once or twice, but that's it. Always be 100% sincere.

Rule #2: Be Frequent: Positive Feedback Once Every 5 Days

Research indicates that the most effective supervisors and managers with the most effective work groups are those who **give each direct report positive feedback at least once every five working days.**

Rule #3: Be Immediate

Which do you think has more impact? Thanking an employee for doing something right the same day they do it; waiting for two weeks; or waiting until performance appraisal time? Right; the sooner, the better.

Rule #4: Be Sure You Give Four Times More Positive Feedback than Performance Feedback

If there's a magic wand in getting performance feedback accepted and acted upon by employees, it's giving them far more positive than performance feedback, in fact, 4:1 positive to performance feedback.

Bosses who communicate what their employees are doing well, and what they need to improve, but who focus more on what they're doing well, get far more cooperation and better results.

What Two Things Are Too Many Employees Told At Work?

1. **They're told what to do.**
2. **They're told what they're doing wrong.**

How motivating are these?

Supervisors and managers often, but not always, get the employees, productivity levels, and work environments they deserve through their use, or lack of use, of positive feedback and performance feedback.

Giving Positive Feedback Skill Practice

Think of an employee who's done a good job (accuracy; speed; at work on time; submits ideas; helped a customer, etc.) and write a script below.

1. **Thank**

_____

_____

_____

_____

2. Tell **WHY**

_____

_____

_____

_____

» Many supervisors and managers think they're giving praise or positive feedback effectively by saying "you're doing a good job," but this isn't sufficient. **It's essential to tell employees WHY they've done a good job.**

The Year Round Performance Improvement System:

Give Employees Performance Feedback Whenever They Need It

+

Positive Feedback Whenever They Earn It

Develop Employees All Year: when you do the above, you'll develop more positive and productive employees all year long instead of trying to cram everything into performance appraisals all at once.

Chapter 14

FAQ: Frequently Asked Questions

Answers to the most commonly asked questions about using these skills.

#1: Do These Skills Work All of the Time?

No.

Nothing I know of works all of the time; nothing is perfect.

However, after developing and using these skills with thousands of managers in different situations in client organizations of different types and sizes, these skills work with most employees most of the time. They're more than likely more effective than what you're using now, plus they give you the best chance of working out something good.

#2: Why Should We Bother Repeating Invalid Concerns Employees Give Us After Using the Check Out Question ("Any concerns about what I'm asking?")

It's to keep you from getting into arguments about whether a concern is valid or not—which will take you off the subject of the feedback (it's one way some employees have learned to manipulate managers so that the real issue doesn't get addressed).

Also, once employees learn that you repeat and answer invalid concerns, they'll usually greatly reduce or stop giving them because such concerns look silly (they often are), plus you haven't gotten sidetracked. In other words, giving invalid concerns no longer works.

In my experience, the single biggest reason employees bring up laundry lists of complaints, excuses, and invalid concerns during feedback sessions is because it's one of the few ways they believe they can resist or exercise any power or choice. (There's a correlation between employee resistance and how well their managers listen to them; resolve concerns; and work with them in general.)

This process gets invalid concerns out of the way, and resolves valid concerns respectfully and far more effectively.

#3: Why Aren't Consequences Included in the Performance Feedback Model?

We're assuming this is the first time the manager has talked with the employee about this situation; bringing in consequences at this point can be needlessly heavy-handed and may suggest that the manager is throwing their weight around.

However—if the infraction is serious enough—or you've already spoken with the employee several times, consequences can be added.

#4: When Do I Stop Collaborating and Insist on a Direction?

After you've used the performance feedback and resolving employee resistance to feedback skills, and believe you've gone as far as you can go.

» **Sometimes you need to insist both of you get back to work:**

"Paul, I've listened to your concerns and mentioned several actions I can take on this. Unless you've got another idea, I need to get both of us back on the production line now."

» **Sometimes you may want to suggest talking at another time:**

"Christina, we've been working on this for 15 minutes, and I think we've gone as far as we can today. Let's both think about it and talk again in 2 days."

#5: Why Should Managers Have to Take the Time and Effort to Do All of This? Why Don't We Just Tell Employees What to Do?! After All, It's What They're Being Paid For!!

It takes additional time to use these skills versus just telling employees what to do.

However, basing manager-employee relationships primarily on the use of authority encourages employees only to do what they have to do to keep their jobs, and no more.

Using these skills improves employee cooperation and performance while reducing resistance, slower work rates, unresolved concerns, and the number of complaints and excuses you're likely to get.

#6: What are the Benefits or Advantages of Using These Skills?

1. **More concerns are resolved with employee input** and participation, making them more committed to achieving solutions.

2. **Using these skills demonstrates that you're genuine** when you say you want improved communication, teamwork, collaboration, the resolution of conflicts, and better work relationships.

3. **More concerns and conflicts are eliminated or resolved** sooner with better solutions.

4. **This is far less confrontational** than other means, and is much less likely to result in unproductive anger and arguments.

5. **Communicating about concerns using dialogue** instead of one-way criticism or demands.

6. **The focus is on shared concerns, collaboration**, problem solving, resolution, and mutual benefit instead on arguing or using authority (which often creates employee resistance).

7. **You're much more likely to learn about the real concerns**, problems, issues and fears your employees have so you can deal with them earlier and more effectively.

   Also, employees are more likely to open up about what's happening in their jobs and the organization on a day-to-day basis, including what they don't understand; what they think is unfair; what they don't know; what they fear; or where they need help by sharing problems that impact their work performance.

   The more you know about such concerns, the better off you, your employees, your organization, and its customers are.

8. **You'll get more ideas** and suggestions for improvements.

9. **Using these skills directly helps develop superior work relationships** with more open communication, information-sharing, respect, trust, rapport, two-way communication, working synergy, and long term employee retention.

#7: Fair is Fair: What are the Disadvantages of Using These Skills?

1. **They take more time** to use.
2. **They take more thinking**, creativity, energy, and problem-solving effort.
3. **You may feel somewhat vulnerable** using them at first.
4. **You're going to have to work to learn them**; practice them; and be willing to try them more than once, more than twice, more than three times, if you don't get the results you want right away.

Do the advantages outweigh the disadvantages?

#8: Doesn't Using These Skills Undermine Managerial Authority?

Actually, I believe they increase respect for managerial authority because managers who use these skills have the intention of working out something good for themselves and their employees, and collaborate with them to do so, a way of working most employees prefer and respond positively to.

In some situations, managers must insist that action be taken; employees are more likely to respect this if their manager has first used a collaborative approach with them whenever possible.

In using all of these skills, managers always reserve the right to make the final decision, and to insist on a course of action.

Working collaboratively with your employees will usually not only improve their performance, it'll also improve your performance in getting things done through them.

#9: Aren't Some Employee Concerns Not Negotiable Using the Resolve Employee Resistance to Feedback Skills?

"I'm thinking about an employee who was wearing flip flops to work in our nursing home. She's required to wear closed toe footwear for safety reasons in case her toes get run over by a wheelchair. I gave her performance feedback; her concern was that she was more comfortable and fashionable in flip flops."

Yes, some things, including safety, legal, ethical matters, and some policies and procedures should not be negotiable when using these skills.

In the situation above, the manager should still respond with the model—Repeat Their Concern; Answer Their Concern> Meet a Standard (safety), but the Action To Take is to insist on enforcing the safety regulations (and being sure others follow them, too).

#10: What If an Employee Interrupts Me While I'm Trying to Give Them Feedback?

You use the first two steps of the Repeat-Answer-Repeat Skill (Repeat Their Concern; Answer Their Concern), then go back to the first step of the Performance Feedback Skill as shown below:

» Set the Stage for Win-Win	"I have a concern I'd like to share with you."

Tell **WHAT** Needs Correcting	"When I see you arrive for work late, past 7:00am..."

Employee	*"What are you talking about, I'm not late, I'm here on time. And how come you're not talking with Rose and Jen, they come in late whenever they feel like it."*

Repeat Their Concern	"What you're saying is you're not late, you're here on time. And that 2 other employees arrive late a lot."

Employee	*"Yes."*

3 Answer Their Concern

» Meet a Standard

"It's important to me that our patients get high quality dental care when they arrive so they don't have to wait for appointments they made months ago and so they come back again."

"It's also important to me that what I'm saying is accurate."

» + Action You'll Take

"I'll review your time cards, and the cards for the other hygienists, for the past 3 months. If I haven't been accurate about this, I'll admit it and will be certain I'm totally accurate in the future."

"If anyone else is arriving late, I guarantee you I'll speak to them, too."

» Go back to Step 1 and begin again.

» If they interrupt you again—some will in order to try to get you off the subject —keep repeating these steps. After several attempts, most employees will see that getting you off track isn't working, and will stop.

That's it.

#11: What About Documenting Feedback Sessions with Employees?

You should follow your organization's policies and procedures about documenting performance feedback conversations with employees. If you're uncertain about them, please contact your Human Resources department or advisor.

#12: What If I Need to Give an Employee Feedback About Something I Haven't Seen Them Do?

Obviously, it's best if you've seen the behavior. If not, structure What/Why #1 this way:

» Set the Stage for Win-Win	**"I have a concern I'd like to share with you."**

Tell **WHAT** Needs Correcting	**"When I hear* that you've been punching in someone else's time card...**

& WHY	**...it lowers morale because everyone isn't being paid fairly for the same time and work."**

Employee	*"Who said that?"*
» Manager	**"Who said this isn't important. What is important is that we're all paid fairly for the same time and work."**

» Rationale: Telling them who said this isn't important—put the focus on what is important, and that is the negative impact their behavior creates. In this case, it's other employees not being paid fairly.

*Other option: "When I understand that you've been punching in..."

Proceed with step 2 of the Performance Feedback skill.

Give Feedback

˅

Get Cooperation

˅

Get Improvement

Appendix A

12 Benefits of Using the "Any Concerns About What I'm Asking?" Step and Question

Some time ago, I was training a group of managers in the How to Give Performance Feedback skill.

They comfortably accepted and followed the model until I got to Step #3, the Check Out step, where the manager asks the employee, "Any concerns about what I'm asking?"

That's when one of the managers quickly and emphatically blurted out, **"Don't go there, Ross!!"**

He went on to say, "If you do, you're just going to get all kinds of excuses, complaints, and a laundry list of gripes. Just shut it off right there, and tell them what to do!"

So I asked the rest of the group:

"What happens if I do this? What happens if I don't ask this question, and just tell the employee what to do?"

One manager said the employee would never open up to me again, never share concerns, and would feel that I wasn't accessible or approachable. In effect, I would shut the employee down forever, she said.

Most of the other managers quickly agreed.

I then asked: "How important is it for managers to listen to employee concerns—even when they're a laundry list of excuses or gripes?"

"Very!" they said.

I also asked: "When would you rather find out about employee concerns, some of them valid, some of them not: now, or later?"

"Now!" they replied.

The group knew that listening to employee concerns was the right thing to do; the one objecting manager feared getting caught up in endless employee excuses without being able to achieve a positive outcome. However, learning how to achieve positive outcomes is what this manual is all about.

It's true that some employees will respond with laundry lists of complaints, often because they have concerns that haven't been fairly addressed; they know they can push their manager off; or because it's one of the few ways they feel they have some power at work.

Believe it or not, the more managers respond to and resolve valid *and* non-valid concerns, the fewer non-valid ones they'll get because employees no longer see a need to bring them up—and because doing so doesn't work when managers know how to respond effectively.

This is what I call a "Critical Relationship Juncture," an exchange between managers and employees that has the potential for a large impact in many areas of their work relationship.

How managers handle feedback sessions with employees is one of the most important "Critical Relationship Junctures" there is, and they occur almost every work week.

Here are 12 benefits to managers of asking "Any concerns about what I'm asking?" and working openly and honestly to resolve them using the skills in this manual.

1. How approachable employees feel their boss is directly affects how much they're willing to share concerns (so they can be answered and resolved in a mutually-beneficial way), and other information.

2. Employees who feel they're listened to, respected, and valued give their bosses far better performance than those who don't.

3. It improves how much employees are willing to collaborate and cooperate about almost any matter or concern.

4. How much employees are willing to improve their job performance: will they perform just good enough to keep their jobs, or will they make improvements so they perform much closer to their full capabilities?

5. The quality and quantity of ideas and improvements they contribute.

6. Their morale, team spirit, attitude, and a whole host of other things we call "work ethic."

7. Their productivity.

8. Reduced absenteeism; requests for transfers to other shifts or departments.

9. Reduced numbers of complaints and grievances, work slowdowns.

10. The manager's own performance in terms of how well s/he leads, manages, and develops employees and their performance.

11. The amount and quality of "working synergy" between employees and managers, and the results *they're* able to accomplish.

12. How long the manager or employer retains the employee; or, put another way, how long the employee retains the employer.

It's amazing how one little question can lead to such big results.

What are Some Other "Critical Relationship Junctures?"

After 25 years of working with individuals, groups, teams, and organizations, here are several others—most of them relatively easy to do or to avoid doing.

1. Not acknowledging employees or calling them by name at the beginning of the work day or when taking visitors on office or plant tours. (This is the single biggest gripe I get from employees!)

2. Not allowing employees to have some input about decisions which affect them.

3. Not giving employees positive feedback when they do things well, even if it's what they're being paid to do.

4. Not giving employees credit for their ideas or suggestions; or, worse yet, taking credit for them yourself.

5. Lying to employees. It's one thing to state something is off limits or you cannot comment on it, it's another to lie; don't.

Managers who successfully navigate these junctures get far better cooperation and performance from their employees.

Give Feedback

ᵛ

Get Cooperation

ᵛ

Get Improvement

A Third Option to Resolve Employee Resistance to Feedback and to Resolve Conflicts

The Skill to Resolve Employee Resistance to Performance Feedback: Repeat-Answer-Repeat

Answer Their Concern Option #3: Both of You Develop a Solution

When employees respond with a concern after the manager asks, "Any concerns about what I'm asking?" in step 3, the Check Out step, here's another way of resolving their concern.

This option can also be beneficial in many conflict resolution situations where more than just feedback is needed.

The Contents of This Chapter
» Answer Their Concern Option #3: Both of You Develop a Solution
» Skill Practice Form

Answer Their Concern Option #3:
Both of You Develop a Solution

When to Use This Skill: *based on the concern the employee gives you,* use this option when a situation is best resolved by the two of you collaborating to develop options and take action, such as an employee not meeting deadlines due to multiple projects with the same deadline.

The Skill to Resolve Employee Resistance to Feedback: Repeat-Answer-Repeat Option #3:

1. **Repeat Their Concern ("What you're saying is...")**
   » No matter what their response is or how valid it is.

2. **Answer Their Concern: Both of You Develop a Solution**
   » **State the Problem**
   » **Brainstorm Options**
   » **Eliminate Options**
   » **Choose a Solution: what each agrees to do**

3. **Repeat What/Why #2**
   » Repeat the What/Why#2 step from the Performance Feedback skill.

» **Here's a new situation; we again begin at What/Why #2:**

Tell **WHAT** You Want Instead	"I'd appreciate it if you'd complete your projects by the deadlines given...
& WHY	...so that other people can incorporate your data and finish their reports on time."
» Check Out	"Any concerns about what I'm asking?"
Employee	"Yes, I can't meet all of my deadlines because there are 3 managers giving me different assignments with the same deadline. Plus, there are other tasks I must complete."

» Here's how the manager responds:

1 Repeat Their Concern

"What you're saying is you're not meeting deadlines because several managers are giving you projects with the same deadline, and you have other work to do."

Employee   "Yes."

» The manager repeats the employee's concern: "What you're saying is you're not meeting deadlines because several managers are giving you projects with the same deadline, and you have other work to do."

This confirms that the manager correctly understood what the employee said; demonstrates to the employee that they've been heard; and helps defuse emotion and build cooperation.

2 Answer Their Concern   » Both Develop a Solution

» State the Problem

"Okay, the problem is how can you meet deadlines for several projects, plus get other work done?"

Employee   "Yes."

» The manager constructs a State the Problem question by mentioning the end results their brainstorming session is to solve: in this case, it's "how can you meet deadlines for several projects, plus get other work done?"

» Brainstorm Options

» Manager	"Okay, let's list some potential solutions on this whiteboard. Let's not evaluate them until we have all of our ideas out so we don't stifle our thinking."
	"I can ask the other managers to coordinate the deadlines on the projects they give you so you're not overloaded."
Employee	*"I could ask Diane or Russ for help if I see that I'm going to get overloaded."*
» Manager	"You could ask Marianne how she handles a number of tasks at once—she's good at it."
Employee	*"Maybe I could take a time management course; I know my skills in this area aren't the best."*
» Manager	"If it looks like you're going to be really busy, let me know ahead of time. I can probably get you a temp."
Employee	*"I could post all of my projects and deadlines so everyone I work with can see them—and check them off when they're completed."*

» Eliminate Options

» Manager	"Ok, we have several ideas. Are there any we can't live with or agree on so we can eliminate them right away?"
» Employee	*"I don't see any."*

» **Manager**	**"Ok, let's choose one or more solutions that'll help you meet deadlines and get work done when there's a lot of it."**
	"How about if I have the other managers communicate so you don't get more than one project with the same deadline?"
Employee	*"That's great. I'll ask Marianne how she handles so many tasks. I'll also ask Diane and Russ for help before I ask you for a temp."*
» **Manager**	**"Good. I'll check with HR about time management courses for you and will approve funding that's $500.00 or less."**
	"These seem good for both of us. Thanks for your help and cooperation."

» The manager:

  » **States the Problem to be Solved:** in this case, it's "Okay, the problem is how can you meet deadlines for several projects, plus get other work done?"

  » **Brainstorms Options:** both the manager and the employee contribute ideas and refrain from evaluating them. Write them down.

  » **Eliminates Options:** options which either feels cannot succeed are eliminated so time isn't spent on unfeasible solutions.

  » **Chooses a Solution/What Both Will Do:** the manager and employee review the solutions; discuss, clarify, and negotiate if necessary, and choose the most effective solution(s).

3 **Repeat What/Why #2:** "I'd appreciate it if you'd complete your projects by the deadlines given...

& WHY ...so that other people can incorporate your data and finish their reports on time."

» The manager repeats (or reasserts) her original request in the Tell What You Want Instead & Why step (What/Why #2) to prompt the employee to agree and move forward.

» In this case, it's **"I'd appreciate it** if you'd complete your projects by the deadlines given...so that other people can incorporate your data and finish their reports on time."

Optional:

» **Confirm If Necessary** "Do I have your agreement?"

Employee *"Yes, I'll get these completed on time."*

» **Thank** "Thanks."

The manager asks if s/he has the employee's agreement if past history suggests the need to confirm agreements with them. If not, skip it

» **Note: you may not need to use Step: Repeat What/Why #2 here** because the employee has already agreed in principle to do what you've asked. It's repeated here to be consistent in showing all 3 steps of this skill.

This Manager and Employee Invested Valuable Time; What Did They Accomplish?

1. The manager found out the real reasons behind the employee missing his deadlines.

2. The solutions they developed are likely better than one(s) the manager would have imposed alone.

3. The two gained skill and a positive experience collaborating together.

4. The employee sees that his manager is willing to give him her best efforts in collaborating with him to resolve concerns in a mutually-beneficial manner instead of making demands. This will likely encourage him to want to resolve future concerns with his manager in the same way.

5. It gives him a higher comfort level with his manager.

6. The two of them are much more likely to resolve other concerns, obstacles, and issues more effectively and comfortably.

» *A Skill Practice form for this skill begins on the next page.*

Skill Practice D: How to Give Employees Performance Feedback AND Resolve Employee Resistance to Feedback: Repeat-Answer-Repeat

Answer Their Concern Option #3: Both of You Develop a Solution

» Write a DIFFERENT feedback situation for the How to Give Employees Performance Feedback Skill below, one that's best resolved by the manager and the employee collaborating to develop options and take action, such as an employee not meeting deadlines due to multiple projects with the same deadline.

» Or, download an interactive template of this form at www.PerformanceFeedback Training.com/skillpractice.

(How to Give Performance Feedback Skill)

» Set the Stage for Win-Win

(Write below: "I have a concern I'd like to share with you.")

Tell WHAT Needs Correcting

"When I...

& WHY

(Why it's a concern; its negative consequence)

84

How to Give Employees Performance Feedback
AND Resolve Employee Resistance to Feedback:
Repeat-Answer-Repeat Option #3 Skill Practice D | Page 1

Tell **WHAT** You Want Instead

"I'd appreciate it if...

& WHY

(Why you want this instead; its positive consequence)

Check Out

(Write below: "Any concerns about what I'm asking?")

(Resolve Resistance to Feedback: Repeat-Answer-Repeat Skill)

Employee's Concern:
(Write a concern an employee might give you in response to the question "Any concerns about what I'm asking?")

Page 2 | How to Give Employees Performance Feedback
AND Resolve Employee Resistance to Feedback:
Repeat-Answer-Repeat Option #3 Skill Practice D

85

1 Repeat Their Concern

(Write down how you'd repeat the employee's concern.)
"What you're saying is…

_____

_____

_____

_____

2 Answer Their Concern: Both of You Develop a Solution

» State the Problem

(What needs to be resolved? For example: "How can you get several projects with the same deadlines done when you have a lot of other work?"
"How can you/we…

_____

_____

_____

_____

» Brainstorm Options

(Write down how you'd suggest both of you develop possible solutions but not evaluate them yet.)

_____

_____

_____

86

How to Give Employees Performance Feedback
AND Resolve Employee Resistance to Feedback: Page 3
Repeat-Answer-Repeat Option #3 Skill Practice D

» Eliminate Options

(Write down how you'd suggest both of you delete options that aren't effective or feasible.)

_____

_____

_____

» Choose Solution(s), Agree on What Each Will Do

(Write down how you'd request both of you choose a solution(s) and discuss and agree about what you'll both do.)

_____

_____

_____

_____

_____

_____

3 Repeat What/Why #2:

(Write your original What/Why #2; it begins with "I'd appreciate it if...")

» *Note: this step often isn't necessary at this point; it's included to consistently show the entire model.*

_____

_____

_____

_____

_____

_____

Page 4 | How to Give Employees Performance Feedback
AND Resolve Employee Resistance to Feedback:
Repeat-Answer-Repeat Option #3 Skill Practice D

87

Optional:

If past history with this employee suggests the need to confirm agreements with them, use this step; if not, skip it.

» **"Do I have your agreement?"** *("Yes.")* **"Thanks."**

88

How to Give Employees Performance Feedback
AND Resolve Employee Resistance to Feedback: | Page 5
Repeat-Answer-Repeat Option #3 Skill Practice D

Appendix C

Matching Employee Concerns with Solutions

Here are several examples of matching Employee Concerns with Options.

Employee Concerns		Option
Not meeting deadlines due to competing priorities	»	Both of You Problem Solve
Employee car problem	»	Facilitate Employee
Uncertain about skills, not getting enough feedback	»	Standard + Action You'll Take
Not following procedures	»	Standard + Action You'll Take or Facilitate Employee
Badmouthing employees	»	Standard + Action You'll Take or Facilitate Employee
Not watching machinery	»	Standard + Action You'll Take or Facilitate Employee
Slow career advancement	»	Both of You Problem Solve
Childcare problem	»	Facilitate Employee
Using cell phone inappropriately	»	Standard + Action You'll Take
Passing off work on others	»	Standard + Action You'll Take

Give Feedback

⌄

Get Cooperation

⌄

Get Improvement

Appendix D

How to Handle Employees Who Give You Multiple Concerns or Excuses After You've Already Used the Check Out Step or Question, "Any Concerns About What I'm Asking?"

Sometimes employees will give you another concern or excuse (or even several of them), after you've used the Skill to Resolve Employee Resistance to Feedback: Repeat-Answer-Repeat.

Every time an employee gives you a concern, respond with the 3 steps in this skill (Repeat Their Concern; Answer Their Concern; Repeat What/Why #2) until you get a resolution.

What if an employee gives me several excuses at once?

Answer them one at a time—using the 3 steps each time—until you get a resolution.

The Contents of This Chapter

Using the Repeat-Answer-Repeat Skill More Than Once to Get a Resolution

Situation: *A foreman is using his cell phone on the shop floor for personal calls, and allowing his employees to do the same.*

Skill Model:	Dialogue Example:
» Set the Stage for Win-Win	"I have a concern I'd like to share with you."
Tell **WHAT** Needs Correcting	"When I see you and other members of your crew talking on cell phones on the shop floor during non-break or lunch periods…
& WHY	"…it means costly production or dangerous safety problems could occur."
Tell **WHAT** You Want Instead	"I'd appreciate it if you and your crew would talk on your phones only during breaks and lunch…"
& WHY	"so that all of us follow the same company rules and avoid errors or accidents."
Check Out	"Any concerns about what I'm asking?"
Employee	*"Yes; other departments do this too, but my department gets more done. A little special treatment like letting my guys use their phones makes this possible."*

» Here's how the manager responds:

Repeat Their Concern	**"What you're saying is that your department gets more done, and having the freedom to make these calls helps motivate and reward your guys. Plus, other departments do this."**
Employee	*"Yes."*

Answer Their Concern	
» Meet a Standard	**"Yes, your department's highly productive, and it produces high quality work, often under difficult deadlines."**
	"It's important that our management team follows and enforces the same rules. As a foreman, you're part of that management team and must follow course."
» + Action You'll Take	**"I promise you that if I see other departments using phones outside of breaks, I'll talk to them right away."**
	"It's important to me to reward good work. How about if you and I meet and brainstorm some ways to recognize your crew that follow company rules?"
Employee	*"Would be ok."*

3 Repeat What/Why #2	"I'd appreciate it if you and your crew would talk on your phones only during breaks and lunch...
	... so that all of us follow the same company rules and avoid errors or accidents."

» **Confirm If Necessary**   "Do I have your agreement?"

Employee   *"Well, what this is really about is you're on my case because you basically dislike me and don't want me to succeed to a higher position in the company."*

» **Now what do we do?** This employee (or foreman) hasn't agreed to the manager's request, and has responded instead with yet another concern!

» **We use the same Repeat-Answer-Repeat Skill again;** in fact, we use it as many times as we get a concern from the employee, and until we get a resolution.

» **Here's how the manager responds:**

1 Repeat Their Concern	"What you're saying is you think I don't like you, and don't want you to be more successful in the company."

Employee   *"Yeah, that's about right."*

» **Asks question to get more information:**   "Please share with me why you think I dislike you and am opposed to your success."

Employee   *"You haven't talked with me about how I can get promoted, what I can do to go to the next level here. And you've done this with others."*

1	**Repeat Their Concern**	"What you're saying is you think I'm not in your corner because I haven't talked with you about how you can advance as I have with some of your peers."
	Employee	*"Yes."*

2	**Answer Their Concern**	
	» Meet a Standard	"It's important to me that I help my people advance. I didn't talk with you about this because I didn't think you were interested." "I apologize for misreading this; I should have pursued it."

	» + Action You'll Take	"Let's you and I meet at least two or three times. We'll discuss your strengths, some things you can improve, and develop an advancement plan for you. Plus, I'll let HR know of your interest." "How does this seem?"
	Employee	*"Sounds good."*

2	**Repeat What/Why #2**	"I'd appreciate it if you and your crew would talk on your phones only during breaks and lunch… so that all of us follow the same company rules and avoid errors or accidents."
	» Confirm If Necessary	"Do I have your agreement?"
	Employee	*"Yes."*

	» Thank	"Thanks."

What the Manager Did and Why:

1. **The manager admitted the foreman's department does a good job.** Many managers would have ignored this, figuring it would only weaken their position by admitting that the foreman's department gets a lot of work completed. This actually strengthens the manager's case; it shows s/he can give credit where it's due, and admitting this helps the foreman listen.

2. **The manager asked a question to get more information.**

3. **The manager was willing to apologize** for a shortcoming; this helps builds credibility and cooperation. Be willing to admit mistakes or shortcomings; they strengthen your argument.

4. **The manager spells out an action s/he can take** on the employee's behalf; repeats What/Why #2, and gets the employee's cooperation.

The Results You'll Usually Get

It may be necessary to **Repeat Their Concern-Answer Their Concern-Repeat What/Why #2** two, three, four, five, even six times. It's hard work.

But where you'll *usually* end up is having your immediate concern resolved; other or hidden issues resolved; and improved communication and cooperation between the two of you.

Do You Want to Improve Feedback and Performance In Your Organization *Now*?

Managers and organizations can get assistance in performance feedback training and coaching to improve their skills and results.

You Can Work with Ross Blake Directly to:

» Resolve difficult or unusual employee feedback situations in your organization.

» Learn any of these skills faster by working with me by phone (or in person).

» Get onsite feedback skills training customized for *your* organization.

» Become certified through a training and approval process to deliver seminars using these skills (corporate training departments and training & development firms).

» Get answers to questions about this book, its skills, or to share successes.

Your Email Gets My Quick Response

To get started, without any obligation whatsoever, just email me at:
Ross@PerformanceFeedbackTraining.com

I'll respond promptly.

If you're inquiring about onsite or telecoaching services, we'll first determine if we're a good fit to work together or not.

If we're not, I'll be upfront and honest enough to tell you.

If we are, you'll control the process every step of the way.

There's no charge for initial consultations, and everything is confidential.

You can improve feedback and performance *now.*

www.performancefeedbacktraining.com

Notes

Notes

CPSIA information can be obtained at www.ICGtesting.com
Printed in the USA
BVOW06s1324270514

354361BV00007B/155/P

How to Give Performance Feedback & *Resolve Resistance*

If you need to give employees feedback about everyday situations, or during performance appraisals, this book was written for you. In addition to learning how to give employees feedback the way they *want* to receive it, and 3 skills to successfully resolve resistance, you'll also learn how to make feedback agreements in *advance* and what to do when employees agree to improve their performance, and then don't. Plus you'll learn real *skills,* not theories.

"If more supervisors and managers learned the helpful skills that Ross Blake teaches in *How to Give Employees Performance Feedback & Resolve the Resistance You Know You're Going to Get!*, the workplace would be much more productive with fewer headaches. Based on solid experience, not theories, these practical skills resolve simple and complex feedback situations at all levels of the organization, and are about as easy-to-read and learn from as possible."

—*Julie O'Mara, President, O'Mara and Associates; Past National President, American Society for Training & Development; Author and Consultant*

"One of the more difficult jobs I had was teaching 35 managers and supervisors the art of giving performance feedback to their subordinates. *How to Give Employees Performance Feedback & Resolve the Resistance You Know You're Going to Get!* offers effective solutions with easy-to-remember procedures. It definitely would have made my job easier."

—*Joseph G. Bellian, Past President, Bicron Corp*

"*How to Give Employees Performance Feedback & Resolve the Resistance You Know You're Going Get!* offers many skills and tips to help managers help employees improve their performance. At the same time, the book suggests several ways to deepen trust and respect in the workplace."

—*Daniel H. Pink, Author of Drive and A Whole New Mind*

"*How to Give Employees Performance Feedback & Resolve the Resistance You Know You're Going to Get!* is a highly positive approach for giving employees feedback without creating defensiveness or resentment, especially for performance issues or behaviors that can't wait until performance reviews are conducted."

—*Jesse Gugino, Director of Continuing Education, State University of New York, Jamestown Community College*

"Supervisors and managers in all types of workplaces can learn how to turn negative performance and behaviors at the time they occur into positive, win-win outcomes with the simple, straightforward, and easy-to-learn skills in *How to Give Employees Performance Feedback & Resolve the Resistance You Know You're Going to Get!*"

—*Linda Hepp, Human Resources Manager (Retired), Alcoa, Inc.*

"If only I'd had this book 20 years ago! It would have saved me (and my employees) countless hours of debilitating, counterproductive stress. In short, easy-to-digest segments, Ross Blake provides managers at every level with a road map to successfully give performance feedback and make good employees even better."

—*Ken Weber, President, Weber Asset Management*

About the Author

Ross Blake is a senior level trainer, a consultant, and speaker. For over 20 years, through seminars, coaching, and consulting projects, he's helped thousands of team leaders, supervisors, managers, HR professionals, and business owners improve their feedback and communication skills in order to improve employee performance and manager-employee work relationships.

"A must-have workbook for anyone who manages or supervises employees on a day-to-day basis. This book easily teaches the essential skills necessary to effectively give performance feedback and deal with resistance in a positive manner."

—*Brian K. Cohen, Vice President, Energy Conservation Partners, LLC*

Give Feedback

⌄

Get Cooperation

⌄

Get Improvement

ISBN 978-0-615-50184-0

90000

9 780615 501840